THE WOMAN IN HAPPY DOLLAR

poems by

Doug McHargue

Finishing Line Press
Georgetown, Kentucky

THE WOMAN IN HAPPY DOLLAR

For all who love going to Happy Dollar

ACKNOWLEDGMENTS

The Fem Literary Magazine and The Hickory Museum of Art Ekphrastic Poetry Reading Series – "Woman Rising"
Dead Mule – "When Dreams Were Dresses"
The Catawba – "Streetscape"
Dimensions –"February Red"
The Best of Hickory Reading Series – "The Power of the Moon", "Dreams Beneath Ice"
Forthcoming *Best of Hickory Reading Series* – "Bag Boy"
The Hickory Museum of Art Ekphrastic Poetry Reading Series – "Run Away"
Wild Goose Poetry Review - "Sugar", "Yellow Bags", "Woman in Happy Dollar", "The Power of the Moon", "Nights at the Dance Club", "Cleopatra of the Catawba", "Men on a Summer Porch"
North Carolina Poetry Society's Poet Laureate Award finalist – "Women Without Make-Up"

Thank You to:

Scott Owens, Joseph Bathanti, Tim Peeler, Richard Allen Taylor, and poet colleagues Ann, Betty, Mel, Patricia, Brenda, Beverly, Kelly, and Nancy; staff of Patrick Beaver Memorial Library in Hickory, staff of Iredell County Library; and to Cameron and Caron McHargue.

Publisher: Leah Maines
Editor: Christen Kincaid
Cover Art: Cameron McHargue
Author Photo: Cameron McHargue
Cover Design: Elizabeth Maines McCleavy

Table of Contents

Sugar

I get in my car,
day after Christmas
budget blown
but leaving Happy Dollar,
woman parked
by the drink machine,
Oh ma'am
Do you have a dollar.
She's not young,
the man beside her
old, in a suit
maybe can't walk
so I go over
they need a soda
and do I have a cup.

I have no cup
but spare change
and desire to get
back on the road
go home, anywhere
but here
and she asks
Do you have sugar.

Packets of sugar, you mean
I ask. *Oh, no, your feet...*
they looked swollen,
straps on my shoes
cutting into my arch
she said like her sister's,
She got sugar.

Sugar, oldtimers' for diabetes.
I say *No*, head for my car
making time.
She goes to the machine
wearing a dress and slow shoes,
sweetness freefalling
through her veins,
not mine.

Yellow Bags

Three women, a girl on the sidewalk
carry Happy Dollar bags,
school bus yellow,
so heavy they're about to burst
leave packs of Charmin,
Preparation H, Gas-X,
Ex-Lax, and Kotex
naked on public streets.

The girl looks up at passing cars
making sure it's not Brandon
third row, second seat English 101
His blondness burns my corneas
or maybe retinas I forget which
we learned that in science
he's in there too
where I want to reach over
Bunson burners and rake
my fingers through that hair
but all he does is stare
at Misty Bridges' bleach job
which made her win
Christmas Queen
and she even knows
what intransitive verbs are
she said so
and I saw her lift her shirt
to Jason Stack under the stairs
but she got to be
Valentine Queen too
which proves something
but I ain't sure just what.

Well anyways it ain't them
gawkin' at me
seein' not only where we been
but how we get there
why do they make
these bags so damn yellow

The Woman in Happy Dollar

Her faded raincoat too thin for January
the woman pushes a shopping cart,
the store's fluorescence casting
unearthly pallor to her face.

I think of John Steuart Curry's painting,
Tornado, his farm woman
clutching baby, running to the cellar
with eyes wide, face green
reflecting a sick sky.

The woman in the store carries her head
like she used to be someone else,
her hair still young but sparse
like her body hanging under the coat,
stains spilled over it
like blurred dreams spoiled.

She looks around wide-eyed
at whatever the world offers
on its shelves, pain's aphrodisiacs,
aspirin, Aspercreme, hair dye, pink nail polish,
and she fills her cart against the storm.

Weeks later I see her
at the grocery, same coat,
hair starving, face
now color of transient angels.
She turns to look at people
next in line as if they
are works of art, safely framed,
her head floating above a body
running ahead of life
before the coat vanishes.

Man outside Happy Dollar

I should know better,
stopping at this store
smashed up concrete
pot hole lot
storm clouds leering
broken people circling.

Do the routine,
get things
run out
before storms
and strangers.

But he's crossing
pot holes, *Hey...Hey*
don't look, just grab
umbrella
run in, run out.
Hey ... How ya doin'
He's no closer
so wave,
wave him away.

He hangs around
the store, I go
inside,tell the clerk
he'll be waiting
but she's heard it all
before and I'm on my own
out those doors
where he sits
on cracked cement
can't even say *Hey*
or stand,

the sky like lead
falling on us, wind
buffeting fools,
twisting umbrella
its spines striking
my back like metal
fingers, bones broken
too many times.

The Dunce Queen of P.E.

I wished I was at a basketball game.
My granddaughter's, that is, in the mountains
but I was stuck in a flatland library,
cloistering walls like an over-protective mother.

In a too dark world I need bright lights
and Happy Dollar. So I left, pulled in
the parking lot, turned on my phone.
It beeped like a fire alarm, my son
texting blow by blow accounts
of the seven-year-old's game.

First text, she'd scored four points
the first minute. Next text, half time
she got all six team points.
Last text, she got the final shot,
would have won the game, but missed.

Still, she gave the Polar Bears all their points,
and I could see her running that seven-year energy
over a full court, trying to figure this out,
help make something come together.
Unlike another girl frozen on a half court
in a fall-down gym, tripping over her own Keds,
laughter stinging her back and now
standing in the paper towel aisle,
tears running down her cheeks,
customers staring, never knowing they're looking
at the Dunce Queen of P.E., vindicated.

Car Whisperer

He knew Mom's car,
how it needed coaxed
a bit more, just not too much.

With teacher-like glasses
he looked at us, swiped
broad hands on a greasy
rag, wanted us to know,
not fear the sighs
and groans of cars.
Hood raised, his ear
heard, hands fine tuned
but could not touch
his heart flying
in the night to some
unnamed rhythm
he said he couldn't count.

That day Mom drove away
praying for all valves,
hands gripping the wheel
steering our life,
her roads time clocks.

I remember hearing he'd died,
thinking he wasn't even
an old man, how he knew
a car's breaths,
who understood *his*,
Mom's drive to work
that morning one long gasp.

When Dreams Were Dresses

Useless Saturday,
the blues washing through me
like an azure river
I drift through town, noisy
palace for rattling souls.

A woman drives past, her passenger
a girl and it's Saturday long past,
mother and me seeking town,
dreams just a dress away.

Careening down little side streets
she drove like we were
flying to the Rapture
my Bass Weejuns pressing floor boards
knowing blue lights and sirens
were only a blink away,
but her eyes, straight ahead
on Gloryland, Spainhour's.

Psyches sated we floated out the store
our car blooming with color
and fabric illusions, an old gray Olds
now Cinderella's carriage
always the dream catcher.

But hitting the highway, she'd poke along
and meeting cars, almost pull over
like the race was finished,
maybe not even won.

She travels now in a wheelchair
both hips broken, ribs cracked,
tendrils in her mind
choking out Spainhour's.

Sometimes she forgets it's me
pushing the chair, becomes
that teacher again
to some lagging pupil, "Come *on*,
come *on*," her hands moving
in circles, little motors.

I pause, talking with a nurse,
mother rolling herself
down the hall in a gray Olds
searching for stray dresses, any beauty.

The Power of the Moon

In October, month of mystery,
an old woman burns a pile of leaves
and behind her, remnants of the sunset,
twilight sky and rising moon.

She leans on a gnarled cane
and turns to stare at me
as smoke rises, offering to appease
a moon who brings in all tides
and pulls babies from wombs.

Sliver of silver, the crescent hoop
worn by the gypsy in Belk's Cloth
and Notions when I was five.
I'd heard when gypsies came to town
clerks had to watch them
for they'd take stuff, steal babies.

But here they were, the gypsy woman
surrounded by sisters and daughters
looking at fabric to sew into dresses
like my mom did, who'd told me
Only loose women wear hoops
in their ears. Then I looked
at the gypsy's dark hair and saw
that crescent moon dangling from her lobe,
orbiting, pulling on us all.

Two Women on a City Bus

Black and white photo,
they sink into seat,
shoulders sloping
toward the millennia.

One speaks the other listens,
knows she will hear
about the dead husband,
how he'd grind yellow teeth
at night, how she hated it,
would give anything
to hear it now, hear babies
cry in the night,
used skin pulls at her chin,
the window behind
an old eight millimeter movie,
sidewalk people and skyscrapers
one and the same,
flesh melding into stone
at the speed of her voice.

K & W Fantasy

She sits in K&W, arm in sling,
bandaged chin, gray hair
strings over a cotton duster.
Three men carry trays,
all round faces, thick necks
football player bodies
gone to flesh, blood pressure
ruling hearts, still a circle,
old woman, center.

The one beside her says
Time for your pill.
She listens to his talk, *She don't*
have to take the pain pill no more.
He looks to his brothers,
She's doing better,
said like a question and we don't
hear the answer, only his voice
louder to her now than the world,
Time for your nerve pill.

She watches stubby fingers
tear open Sweet 'n Low,
sprinkle sparkling powder
into her tea, fairy dust drifting
over long blond curls.

February Red

Gray tangles, like an old woman's hair
twisted and knotted
when she rises from an unslept bed,
spread a dull blanket
of dead kudzu
over sapless trees.
A faint red edges the tips
of one young tree,
and if the old woman saw it
she would remember the color
her lips used to be.

Women without Make-Up

Mornings my hair hangs haggard,
skin blotched, dark circles
like women of Appalachia
beat up by years.

The woman's photo shows
faded strings for hair
against a white dove face
bones for elbows, baby at breast
toddlers pulling her skirt
from the Jesus Saves truck,
two sizes too big.
She speaks sharp to the kids
a dragged out, raw drawl
like she's had little school,
echos of Old English.

Her color means no fruit
but lots of starch
save some for the babies
leave me alone to the husband
By God I will
bones jumping out her skin,
curses, but she gives
each bird a name.

My hair like straw,
no mascara, bags for eyes,
a man just waking will stir his coffee,
carefully not looking my way,
and when he walks out
never learns birds eat out of my hand.

Red Nile

Surging against veins
my pressure rises
with the ebb and flow
of my life
sweeping to old shores
where women have always waited
for men to come home,
kiss their shaking lips.

Sisters of solitude we fear
that water`s edge
where we can slip,
nobody to throw us a rope
pushed by currents
uncontrollable as blood
that red river cutting its path,
tributaries branching out
through flaying arms,
gushing to our fingertips
spilling into the Nile
where Cleopatra floated
and even with her Mark Antony
still had to appease the gods.

Run Away

She runs toward the truck
with its secret driver
at the picture's edge,
her dress ruby stained
as the day she first bled.

Behind her, red hen white hen,
sheets on the line
one white one scarlet,
her spirit hanging.

How we lay down brooms
leave jobs and hats
and family at table
run to that shining white truck,
and it's always driven
by angels, shrill with siren songs.

Rain on Times Square

School trip to New York
I strayed, looked down
marble hotel stairs,
Alice down the rabbit hole
to some club, little tables for two,
precarious seats for this country girl.

Afraid, I only peered
at secret depths, whiskey
corners, deep stained bar.
As the sixties played out
I should've slid down
those steps, learned to swallow
Manhattans by day,
slept on the bar at night,
had my chasers in the morning.

It seemed a jazz trio
was on the edges, long low notes
sobbing to rain on Times Square
as a couple kissed,
now even holding hands my regret,
quicksilver rain heavy
like mercury combing their hair.

Nights at the Dance Club

You flat out left me
on this flat plane of earth
so I went dancing.
He danced light and easy
with witty repartee`
and asked me out,
but cutting into filet mignon
no vodka in hand
his throat went to gravel
smothering all words,
feet turning to clay.

I went out with another,
his dancing intense
as his love for an ex,
seeing her
while seeing me,
platitudes slipping
from each side of his mouth.

But I'd go every Friday
even dancing with a young Elvis,
his scarves, wrinkled as the women
who caught them, flying
over the dance hall like little flower colored
parachutes of hope.

Soft lights and shoulders to lean against,
music live and loud
giant revolving ball glittering
on middle-aged sallowness
like sequined make-up
we'd wear on a carrousel
going round and round the room
hanging on to each other
so we don't fall off the earth.

Dreams beneath Ice

Home at dark from a trip
I look out my glass door,
all of heaven's clouds
descended over brown grass
covering all sins
the ground silent
about how it's scarred,
pacified by sweet white.

But how its sweetness played us for the fool,
my thinking it brought us together
you shoveling my driveway
like we'd find something,
little epiphanies lying everywhere
beneath ice.

I watched your bootprints
turn to slush,
then become the air.

Then I let snow fall on me
like little dove feathers
brushing against a sliced soul,
my cement cherub's icicle-grounded
wings safe as a museum piece
under glass.

TV said a woman left
for work this morning,
skidded off the road
in a pond, into the glassy dreams.

Cleopatra of the Catawba

Her back a young tall column
and the raft a vinyl barge
the woman reigns,
the boy paddles up river,
photo-shooting spiders.

Camera strapped to her chest
she holds her head regally
but stiff as Egyptian drawings,
Cleopatra exploring small beasts' worlds,
comparing their web to hers.

The boy is movement
his muscles pushing the raft
but silent as Cleopatra's slave
who thinks if he throws down the oar
and dives in, how he will
open the waters.

Men on a Summer Porch

The apartments sit where an old house was,
Victorian porch wrapped all around,
white railings cradling
but not saving it.

These porches are tiny and cement,
men with bronze hands sitting there,
grasping grocery bags of lunches
Spanish words telling how
bossman's lettin' twenty go
and *maybe we gotta go back,*
two of them on a narrow bench
sweaty work clothes touching,
uncomfortably close
backs stiff against wood
like prim arthritic ladies
out on a warm afternoon
taking tea together
in bone china cups,
sitting on the edges of truth.

Bag Boy

Bagger on break
he rushes out the grocery,
looking for the girl.

She leans on her car
like the most casual thing
she's ever done is date
this spare-change smiling blue collar.
Red hair flicking like flames
she throws back her head,
cigarette between fingers
like more worldy women
used to tuxedo men
offering up the lighter,
sacrificial fire.

She's already inhaling
as he runs across
freedom's parking lot,
racing to embrace what makes
his fingers shake
then stands in her shadow,
hears how full of crap
the day's been
ain't no boss
gonna tell me
what to do
and when he starts filling shelves
he sees auburn hair sweeping
his life, cans of corn lined
up like soldiers.

Regrets

They called them Walldogs.
Ladders leaned on stores,
they painted red mouthed
laughter, women lifting Cokes
toasting the good life.

Word was, if you paint, you drank.
Answers in bottles, in hand,
on walls big enough
to pay the rent.
Mural size teeth
three coated white, balloon
size bubbles all around
a no-regrets smile,
drink this.

Last of lips brushed
the painters rode to big houses,
spread buckets of beige,
tight cheeked women
straight lines for lips
hissed, *You missed a spot.*

Tall doors shut
they faced sunset
lavender swiping sky,
wanted to keep it splash it
all over something, forever color
but were nothing but bristles, bent.

Streetscape

I sit streetside
a fancy table
but diesel perfume,
the music, pistons, gears
metal on metal
big white Lincoln metal
driver's white hairdo
big as the car,
on sidewalk small woman
on phone in foreign tongue,
in the tongues of angels
for all I know.

Runners running
from tongues, talk, faces
who face plate glass
window shopping
no money,
woman in car shopped,
bought living room,
sofa strapped to roof
chairs in trunk,
driver rigid, can't see
hopes nobody stops fast.
Old gray pick-up roars
to stop, parks,
two teens near, bodies
spilling from leggings,
mini skirts, one cries
God, I love his truck

He gets out
they love him, too
for he's a hunk
sees nothing but phone
and they start their run,
large hearts panting,
sweat dripping from glands
deep as wells
they turn the corner,
runaways disappearing
into adulthood.

Crazy Air

Friday air smolders
on the sidewalk, two guys
bodies so jumpy
they can't hold trouble,
girl with baby beside them
like afterthoughts.

One rushes to the street,
skin grey
parchment, inked
jerky movements
cadence cursing
shaved head rapper
screaming into cars.

Tall, dreadlocked, the other
in an arm cast shakes it
at the car ahead,
my foot slamming brakes.

The driver silent but not
silly moves on, all
to steamier sets as I drive
into crazy southern air,
melting asphalt,
grocery lots with people
who yell over my head,
man with wet washrag
over his, carrying take-out
pizza too hot to touch,
eat, woman at the grocery
heading to parking lot,
a couple wait, sweat at their necks,
she lags on purpose
pushing cart but hearing
Ave Maria, how it once
floated from her throat
to high holy rafters.

At Social Security

we wait, chair bodies, plastic hard.
Thick arms push open glass doors,
purple shoes first thing
you see, modest heels but suede,
color of her dress, color of rich,
Bible royalty,
says to giver of numbers,
Clay pot out there –
painted my house that color,
stares like it is far away.
Number giver says, *Must've been*
lots of work.

Oh yessir but pretty.
It burned down.
She sits, looks outdoors.

Number called, she rises
on stiff legs, purple heels
smothering ashes.

Woman at my Car

Fallen through every crack,
she's landed at my car
this plaid shirtdress woman,
aged cheekbones like a sculptor
took brown clay, molded
it to high purpose,
glasses on her nose like a teacher
who'd listened to circles of kids,
red birds, blue birds
and the yellow birds
who read *dog* backwards,
saw it as *god*, and she smiled.

She points to misshapen feet,
swollen fingers, says she can't make
co-pays, owns home
so agencies look away,
she looks at me
fingering twenties for gas,
groceries, a big bill month.

Too softly, she says *Now don't do it
if it hurts* as I rifle through
spare change, coins clanking
loud as closed doors.

She thanks me, me of small hands,
but big gripes, health care,
insurance, state of the union,
just talk, as I head into the library
looking for a book with answers.

Woman Rising

You can see swipes
the artist made getting mud
on canvas, skin for this woman
maybe like God stretched
clay and dust over a bunch of bones
to get his man.

But this woman stares at us
a hint of irony about the eyes,
her head tilted a bit,
and pushing up by her elbows
rises from clay herself
thank you very much,
not from some old used rib

Pay Day

Friday afternoon America
in Happy Dollar,
men in Wranglers, pockets stuffed
with paychecks,
carrying plastic baskets,
Tide for greasy spots leaked
on blue collars by machines
running their lives.

They come in by themselves,
no woman to say which soap
is best, mothers on farms,
barren wheatfields
where grandfathers turned soil
in bib overalls
left in those fields forever.
These men wear jeans
on Sundays.

I see them go from shelf to shelf
quickly deciding which paper towel
best wipes up beer
spilled in a dim room
where t.v. is the light.

Alone too, I watch them
pass up ceramic angels
with flowing blue dresses
and blond hair.
One has eyebrows raised
like she is surprised to be here
among dish rags and Draino.
Another looks like Jean Harlow
with red lips pouting
in the style of the day
when my grandmothers lived
and believed heaven was full of angels,
so I buy both of them.

Doug McHargue has worked in a truck terminal, a dress shop, and served as a file clerk, Avon salesperson, receptionist, newspaper feature writer and public school teacher, and is grateful for the life lessons these experiences gave her.

She is published in *Wild Goose Poetry Review, Kakalak 2016, Kakalak 2017, The Dead Mule, Bloodshot, The Fem Literary Magazine, The Best of Poetry Hickory Reading Series, The Catawba,* and *Dimensions.* She was a 2014 finalist for the North Carolina Poetry Society's Poet Laureate Award.

Raised on a farm in Iredell County, North Carolina, she attended Mitchell College and is a graduate of Appalachian State University. She now lives in Catawba County where she is a regular reader at both Poetry Hickory and the ekphrastic Art of Poetry series at the Hickory Museum of Art.

www.ingramcontent.com/pod-product-compliance
Lightning Source LLC
LaVergne TN
LVHW051612080426
835510LV00020B/3259